THE BENJI METHOD

Teach Your Dog to Do What Benji Does in the Movies

Joe Camp

Second Edition

Also by Joe Camp

The Soul of a Horse
Life Lessons from the Herd

The Soul of a Horse Blogged
The Journey Continues

Who Needs Hollywood
The Amazing Story of a Small Time Filmmaker
Who Writes the Screenplay, Raises the Production Budget,
Directs, and Distributes the #3 Movie of the Year

Coming

Born To Be Wild
The Soul of a Horse

The Soul of a Happier Healthier Horse
No Stalls - No Shoes - No Sugar

For more: www.14handspress.com

Published in the United States by 14 Hands Press,
an imprint of Camp Horse Camp, LLC

www.14handspress.com

Library of Congress Control Number: 2011902201

Library of Congress subject headings

Camp, Joe; Motion Pictures

Benji

Human-animal relationships

Human-animal communication

Dogs --Training

Dogs --Behavior

ISBN 9781930681279

Second Edition

What Readers and Critics Are Saying About Joe Camp

"Joe Camp is a master storyteller." THE NEW YORK TIMES

"Joe Camp is a gifted storyteller and the results are magical. Joe entertains, educates and empowers, baring his own soul while articulating keystone principles of a modern revolution in horsemanship." RICK LAMB, AUTHOR AND TV/RADIO HOST "THE HORSE SHOW"

"This book is fantastic It has given me shivers, made me laugh and cry, and I just can't seem to put it down!" CHERYL PANNIER, WHO RADIO AM 1040 DES MOINES

"One cannot help but be touched by Camp's love and sympathy for animals and by his eloquence on the subject." MICHAEL KORDA, THE WASHINGTON POST

"Joe Camp is a natural when it comes to understanding how animals tick and a genius at telling us their story. His books are must-reads for those who love animals of any species." MONTY ROBERTS, AUTHOR OF NEW YORK TIMES BEST-SELLER THE MAN WHO LISTENS TO HORSES

"The tightly written, simply designed, and powerfully drawn chapters often read like short stories that flow from the heart. Camp has become something of a master at telling us what can be learned from animals, in this case specifically horses, without making us realize we have been educated, and, that is, perhaps, the mark of a real teacher." JACK L. KENNEDY, THE JOPLIN INDEPENDENT

"This book is absolutely fabulous! An amazing, amazing book. You're going to love it." Janet Parshall's America

"Joe speaks a clear and simple truth that grabs hold of your heart." YVONNE WELZ, EDITOR, THE HORSE'S HOOF MAGAZINE

"I wish you could hear my excitement for Joe Camp's new book. It is unique, powerful, needed." DR. MARTY BECKER, BEST-SELLING AUTHOR OF SEVERAL CHICKEN SOUP FOR THE SOUL BOOKS AND POPULAR VETERINARY CONTRIBUTOR TO ABC'S GOOD MORNING AMERICA

"I got my book yesterday and hold Joe Camp responsible for my bloodshot eyes. I couldn't put it down and morning came early!!! Joe transports me into his words. I feel like I am right there sharing his experiences. And his love for not just horses, but all of God's critters pours out from every page." *RUTH SWANDER – READER*

"I love this book! It is so hard to put it down, but I also don't want to read it too fast. I don't want it to end! Every person who loves an animal must have this book. I can't wait for the next one !!!!!!!!!" *NINA BLACK REID – READER*

"I LOVED the book! I had it read in 2 days. I had to make myself put it down. Joe and Kathleen have brought so much light to how horses should be treated and cared for. Again, thank you!" *ANITA LARGE - READER*

"LOVE the new book… reading it was such an emotional journey. Joe Camp is a gifted writer." *MARYKAY THUL LONGACRE - READER*

"I was actually really sad, when I got to the last page, because I was looking forward to picking it up every night." *SABINE REYNOSO - READER*

"*The Soul of a Horse Blogged* is insightful, enlightening, emotionally charged, hilarious, packed with wonderfully candid photography, and is masterfully woven by a consummate storyteller. Wonderful reading!" *HARRY H. MACDONALD - READER*

"I simply love the way Joe Camp writes. He stirs my soul. This is a must read book for everyone." *DEBBIE K - READER*

"This book swept me away. From the first to last page I felt transported! It's clever, witty, inspiring and a very fast read. I was sad when I finished it because I wanted to read more!" *DEBBIE CHARTRAND - READER*

"This book is an amazing, touching insight into Joe and Kathleen's personal journey that has an even more intimate feel than Joe's first best seller." *KATHERINE BOWEN – READER*

Preface

Over the years, to the date of this writing, three different Benjis have starred in five theatrical motion pictures and numerous television programs. All of them, including the current Benji, have been trained using the concepts in this book, what we now call *The Benji Method*. Worldwide, more than 75 million people have watched Benji movies in theaters and over a billion have watched Benji on television. And pretty much all of them have fallen in love with our floppy-eared mutt because of the uniqueness of incorporating compassion and true communication into the training process. It shows on the screen and will show in your relationship with your dog.

If you haven't seen our online video *Benji Movie Memories* I recommend that you do before beginning this book because I believe it will get you excited about the good times in store for you and your dog. It's a three-minute video with clips from all five Benji movies starring all three different Benjis. And your dog will soon be doing everything that Benji does. The link: *http://www.thebenjimethod.com/BenjiMovieMemories.htm* (case sensitive).

Joe and Benji on the set of *Benji off the Leash*

INTRODUCTION

This book, and the Video of the same name, dispels the notion that training your dog is difficult, or must be done by an expert, or that you need an encyclopedia of historical and/or psychological knowledge to even try.

Training your dog is simply a matter of love and logic. And real communication. And patience. The purpose of this book is to make you your own dog's best trainer. To make you comfortable with that fact so you will be able to have terrific communication with your dog throughout his or her life. Without a bunch of experts telling you that you *must* do it their way.

It's really that simple. Common sense and compassion. You start by loving your dog, and being a good and trusted companion. Dogs want to please. They strive to please. You need only give them the opportunity in a structured environment, in a manner your pup can understand. If you take each one of the exercises in this book, in sequence, and work with your dog every day, soon she will be able to do a lot of what Benji does in the movies; but more importantly she will rapidly begin to understand *the process*, and then virtually anything is possible. It's all about building a foundation, and then building upon that foundation. That's why everything *must* be taken in sequence. Follow the sequence and soon your pup will understand that when you speak to her it has meaning and she will be stretching to grasp that meaning, and to apply it. You will have an understanding of how to communicate with her; and how to extend her learning throughout her lifetime. Your dog will understand you and your wishes better, be controllable, and you'll both be a lot happier because she has a defined way to please you.

Some dogs will pick up these exercises quickly, others will take longer. Dogs are like us. Some are brilliant, some aren't. Some are stubborn, some aren't. Some are mischievous. Some aren't. The personalities of a Jack Russell Terrier and Benji are quite different. All of this plays into the learning curve. Over the years, I've had many folks say, "Gee, I wish my dog was as smart as Benji." My answer is always the same. "Odds are he or she is." But those pups have never been asked to do everything that Benji is asked to do. Most dogs never have the opportunity to receive the extensive training that Benji gets. And with dogs – again, just like people – the more they learn, the faster they learn, and the better they get at it. And the more they learn, the more they *want* to learn. It becomes exponential.

I have no idea how this book compares to other books and other methods of training because, frankly, most of the ones I've picked up are very tedious, and I never finish them. Not to say the methods are bad or wrong, it's just that training a companion animal is not academic, it's personal; and it's not rocket science. If the love, and thus the motivation, is there, it becomes very much a matter of developing communication by simply putting one foot in front of the other, i.e.: common sense.

Logic.

The content herein is not meant in any way to be a training guide for show animals. I know nothing about the show ring and all that goes on there. This book is designed for folks who love their companion animals and want to give them, not unlike children, an environment in which there can be communication, understanding, structure, compassion, growth, and trust. My experience is not academic. It was not learned in a classroom. It has come from more years than I care to admit spent watching Frank Inn, one of the world's greatest trainers for movies, do his thing; and taking his compassion, his logic, his methods and applying them to my own dogs. And to Benji #3.

By necessity, much of what you'll find here relies on vocabulary. And comprehension of concept. Not mechanical rote memory training. The concept for Benji movies revolves around the dogs being the emotional center of the story, not the people. In pre-Benji dog movies, for example, your heart was with the kid who had to get rid of the dog because he was eating the chickens. The dog was more or less a prop. In the Benji movies, your heart is with the dog and his struggle to overcome something that is very difficult for a real dog to accomplish. In a Benji movie, the *people* are the props. The dog must *act*. Express emotion. That's why I call it *trial-and-error* film making. We often don't know exactly what we're going to do when the cameras roll until we're on the set doing it. Or, often, what we planned to do simply doesn't work out so we have to change and re-design on the spot. We, therefore, must be able to talk to Benji, point out what needs to be done, and have her understand. That might sound bizarre to Pavlovians, but that's the way we do it, and it works. And that's what you'll be doing soon.

One other thing I should explain: I'm not a professional trainer. I do not do it for a living. But I am a student of what works. Logic and common sense to a fault, I suppose. When Benji is preparing for a movie, she spends most of her time with a professional trainer. Genny Kerns, in the case of the recent, *Benji Off the Leash.* Genny trains for a living, and like Frank Inn before her, she subscribes to and uses the very same concepts used in this book when she is working with Benji. And she's very good at what she does. A note of trivia: Genny actually worked for Frank back before the original Benji was made, when Higgins, the dog who played Benji in the first movie, was working on a television show called *Petticoat Junction*. Genny was Higgins' trainer on the set. So, in a way, she has come full circle by training both the original *and* Benji #3. Thanks Genny. And thanks also to Roger Schumacher who trained Shaggy (aka Lizard Tongue) and Benji's mom in that movie.

But back to *your* dog. When you have been through this entire regimen with your pup, if you have paid as much attention as your pup has, you will, like me, be able to teach your dog just about anything that makes sense, developing your own ways to communicate as you go, because the training will be based upon logic, communication, and comprehension of concept. Not rules, or rote memory training. Not Pavolvian responses. The primary purpose of this book is to give you the understanding and tools to keep building your dog's vocabulary throughout her life. Yes, *vocabulary!* And as her vocabulary grows, she will be able to put those words together into differing phrases and sentences, just like a learning child. She will have the communication skills to understand the very nuances of your wishes. Which will bring you and your dog closer to each other, and that can only be a very good thing.

If you have any problems understanding the hand signals or the lessons contained in this book, please refer to the Video of the same name. See the last page of this book.

FOREWORD

Benji #3 was picked up by Animal Control on the back streets of Pass Christian, Mississippi, abandoned, lost and alone, and wandering aimlessly. She was taken to the Humane Society of South Mississippi in Gulfport. About that time I was flying to the Mississippi Gulf Coast to meet another dog in the same shelter. We were on a national search for the new Benji in shelters all across the country and we had been sent photos of a pup named Jodie who had been picked up in Gulfport. Jodie was very much a Benji look-alike and I needed to see the dog first hand. When we arrived at the Gulfport PetSmart where the Humane Society regularly displays pets for adoption, Eric Aschaffenburg, Interim Director of the Society, sprung a surprise on me. He not only showed me Jodie, the dog we had come to see, but surprised me with the pup who had been picked up in Pass Christian. I immediately fell in love.

On November 18, under the watchful cameras of ABC's *Primetime Thursday*, my wife Kathleen and I adopted that pup and she flew with Kathleen, to our home in north San Diego county to meet up with two other candidates, one adopted from Chicago's Animal Care and Control shelter, and one from the Carson Shelter near Los Angeles.

The three spent a week with our family, then a week with a professional trainer. Then a selection was made. The entire search was followed by ABC News and the ultimate selection

11

was announced on ABC's *Primetime Thursday,* and then the new Benji and I appeared live on *Good Morning America* in ABC's New York studios the next morning.

Here was a dog who, as far as we knew, had never been out of southern Mississippi, and she took to New York life like she was born there, completely unaffected by the noise, the traffic, or the crowds of the big city at Christmastime. The only thing that seemed to bother her is the idea of being left alone. It was as if she were afraid we might not come back. A leftover, most likely, from being abandoned back in Mississippi. So, except when she's at home with all the other dogs, we don't leave her alone. Haven't to this day.

The mystery to me, is why *any*one would ever abandon this dog. We love her so much we have trouble letting her go back to a trainer to prepare for a film.

The *original* Benji was rescued from the Burbank Animal Shelter and the American Humane Association says that fact is directly responsible for the adoption of more than 1,000,000 dogs around the country. That's why we wanted to find the new Benji in a shelter. To help raise that number of adoptions even higher. And, now, every time someone looks into those big brown eyes they are seeing the kind of love they, too, can find by adopting a pet from their local shelter. To be at least partially responsible for so many animals being saved is one terrific feeling.

For more about Benji, see the Appendix or the last page of this book. But now, grab your leash and your favorite canine and let's get to work.

LESSON ONE: THE BASICS

HAND SIGNALS

When training for the movies, a hand signal always goes along with a verbal command. You can probably guess why. When shooting a scene for a movie, often the actors working with the dog have lines to say and those lines cannot be ruined by a trainer speaking commands to the dog. So, as the dog learns each new thing, he learns it both by *hearing* the instruction, *and seeing* the hand signal... so eventually the trainer only needs to use the hand signal, *without any verbal command*, and the dog gets the idea. Therefore, all of our training tips will involve both verbal commands *and* hand signals. The advantage to you is that once your pup is used to hand signals, sometimes a mere point or tilt of the head is enough to obtain the desired result. Comes in handy when you're in conversation, or on the phone, or just showing off how smart your dog is. For example, I can point to the sofa and flick the jump signal, and Benji knows exactly what to do. She trots over and jumps onto the sofa without a word being spoken. One of our dogs is older and is almost deaf, but a loud clap of the hands to get her attention, then a hand signal, and she'll still perform her entire repertoire.

THE REWARD SYSTEM

Always work on the reward system. Never use punishment. Find a treat that your dog likes and give him one (a tiny one) *every* time he does what you ask him to do... but don't stop there.

Praise him! A lot! Act very excited that he did what you wanted. Show him you love him! Soon he will *want* to do what you ask because dogs, like people, love to be praised. Scratch him behind his ears. Pet him on his head. But never, ever scold him or punish him when he doesn't do what you ask. Never. Keep all training *positive* and you'll be amazed how well it works.

Be Consistent

Training takes time. Especially in the beginning. Don't start unless you're willing to spend periods of time at least ten or fifteen minutes long, at least twice a day, preferably three times a day. *Every* day! There is no magic button you can push to suddenly have your dog doing some of the cool stuff you'll learn here. You have to work with your dog on a regular, consistent basis. It's mileage, mileage, mileage. The good news is that it can be fun, for you, and especially your dog. He'll look forward to the sessions because he likes to please you and he likes to be praised. But don't expect these good results if you only work with him once or twice a week, or just whenever *you* feel like it. Be consistent. That also means: always say the commands the same way and use exactly the same hand signals. Don't change things. At least, in the beginning. You'll confuse your dog.

Avoid Distractions

Always do your training alone, in a quiet setting, just you and your dog. It's very important that she pay strict attention to you. If other people are in the room, she'll be looking to them for attention as well as you, and she won't be paying as much attention to you. If other dogs are around, she'll likely want to play. Also, don't try to show other people what your dog is learning

14

until she has fully learned it. Has it down pat. Can do it in her sleep. Then you and your dog won't be frustrated and you won't be disappointed when the two of you show off.

SIT AND STAY

These could be the two most important things you will teach your dog. Why? Because to teach the more difficult stuff you must have absolute control over your dog, and you won't have that control until he has learned to sit and stay… in one spot… *until you tell him he can move…* no matter how long that might be… no matter where you might go. Even if you leave the room. Even if you're in the middle of Times Square on New Year's eve! So let's get started.

"SIT"

Even if your dog already knows how to sit, you might want to teach her again so she'll get used to the hand signals… and so she will understand that the "stay" command is virtually a part of the "sit" command. After a while, she will understand that when you tell her (or motion her) to sit, she should stay right there until you tell her differently.

You will need your dog's leash and some treats. The treats should be tiny, just a taste, because you don't want to break up the training session while your dog chews up an entire dog biscuit. Too, if she gets full, she will lose interest, *and* she might not eat her regular meal, which is another reason you keep the training sessions short. Also, you don't want it to become too much of a chore, or tiring, for you *or* your dog. You want to keep it fun.

1. First attach the leash to your dog's collar.

2. Walk far enough away to cause your dog to stand on all four feet if he happens to be sitting.

Then, walk slowly toward your dog, shortening the leash as you go, until you're right over the dog's head.

As you take the last step, hold the leash high and tight (not pulling on the collar, but with no slack in it, so the dog cannot step back or away from you). Point toward the dog's tail and say "Sit."

Often this works the very first time. Here's why: Most dogs do not like to bend their necks backward to tilt their heads back so they can look straight up at you when you are standing right above them. It's much more comfortable for them to sit down to look up at you. If this doesn't work the first time, keep talking to the dog (saying "sit") while you lean even further over him (keeping all slack out of the leash). He *will* eventually sit down. Just be sure you're saying "sit" and pointing to his tail when he does. Then go bezerk with praise! "What a good dog! Such a smart puppy!" Show him that you mean it, and give him a treat. Then after a bit, get your dog on his feet, walk away, and do the whole thing again... walking toward the dog... shortening the leash... pointing to his tail... and saying "sit." The minute he does, praise him lavishly and give him another treat.

Do this eight or ten times. Then, when you get the feeling that the dog is beginning to understand... don't walk quite so close, but give the hand signal (pointing toward his tail) and say "Sit." If he does, then you can back off even a bit more and do the same thing. If he doesn't quite have it yet, get closer again so he has to sit to look up at you.

Once he gets the idea, and you no longer have to stand right over him, you can try it without the leash. Always remembering to "pay" your dog with love, praise, and a treat every time he sits.

A word about the hand signal. I said you should point to your dog's tail but in reality it should be more than just a "point." Make a motion out of it, like your hand is rolling over the top of a circle or a ball, your pointing finger sort of moving toward the dog's tail. Dogs, just like all of us, pay more attention to things in motion than stationary objects.

The real lesson at work here: Frank Inn, Benji's original trainer, always said the best training starts with something the dog does naturally and teaches her to associate a hand signal, a command, praise, love, and a treat with that behavior. In this case, the dog will sit naturally when you tower over her so she can look up at you more comfortably. And gradually she will understand that's what you want when you say "Sit" and give her the hand signal. But she's also learning more: that your command and the hand signal are associated with a desired action. She will grow to understand this. So the next command and hand signal will come easier, more quickly. Because she's now getting the picture that when you give a command with a hand signal, then praise her and give her a treat that she's supposed to repeat.

With the sit command, there could be a problem if the trainer is too short and the dog is too big for the "tower" effect to work. In that case, the trainer might have to stand on a step-stool (to get a bit taller), or ask a parent to help.

Once your dog is sitting <u>every</u> time you say "sit" (and point to her tail), you can move on to the "stay" command... but don't even start the next section until your dog sits every time you tell her to.

"STAY"

This one is more difficult, because it asks the dog to do something that most dogs do not do naturally, something they do not *want* to do. If you walk away from your dog, he usually wants to come with you, right? And what you're now about to ask him to do is something he naturally doesn't want to do... but, once he understands that it's something you want him to do, and that he can please you by doing it, and you'll give him love and praise and treats for doing it, he will *then want* to do it for you. And remember, with each new thing you teach your dog, he will be understanding more and more that when he does what you want, he gets praised and gets a treat, so he'll begin to try even harder.

Tell your dog to sit (using the hand signal). Then begin to say "Stay!" over and over, pointing the flat palm of your hand toward the dog's nose, as if it was a barrier... then very slowly, take one step backward. If the dog stays, keep up the verbal and hand commands, and take one more step backward. If the dog continues to stay after two steps back, become excited, and say "Okay! Come here. Good boy! What a good dog!" and give him a treat. If the dog does not stay when you take the first or second step backward, say "No, no. Stay." Have the dog sit, and start over. Place the flat palm of your hand right in front of his nose if necessary so that it actually *is* a barrier. Be firm of voice. Don't scare or confuse him, but let him know by the tone of your voice that he should *stay*. Then take a step back, palm out, saying *stay* over and over.

Once it's working, then slowly, ever so slowly, stretch it to three steps backward before you call him... then four steps... then six... then ten. Take it in small increments. Do *not* rush it. Always praise the dog and heap love on him every time he gets it right. Remember, this is not a natural act for the dog. He wants to come with you. He has to learn, slowly, that he can please you by not coming when you say "Stay" and use the hand signal.

Before too long, you should be able to cause your dog to sit and stay without saying a word, just using hand signals. Eventually (and this will take a while longer) you should even be able to leave the room (while saying "Stay...stay.") and when you walk back in, your dog will still be sitting right where you left her. When you get to that point, pat your dog on her head and yourself on the back. Only then should you go on to Lesson Two.

A Word About Crate Training

We currently have five dogs. All are crate-trained. For me, it's the only way. Some folks seem to think it's cruel to lock a puppy up in a crate. Not so, and you'll see why as you read on. I first learned to crate train from Frank Inn, Benji's original trainer. He was definitely an advocate. The procedure is quite simple but takes some discipline on your part, especially when your dog is a puppy. We always use foldable wire crates, sized to the dog in question. Too big is as wrong as too small. The crate should be large enough for comfort, but small enough to be cozy. A little nest. The concept is that most dogs will *not* soil their bed, their nest. So it's the best way to teach a pup to hold it until the appropriate potty area is available We like to use wire crates so the dogs can see all that's going on around them, but Frank always used the standard heavy plastic shipping crate.

Start immediately, if possible, the day you bring your new puppy home. This method will work with older dogs too, but the earlier the better. Take your puppy outside, to whatever place you would like her to relieve herself, and put her down. If she does her duty, go bezerk with praise! And play with her for a short while. Let her explore a bit. Maybe thirty minutes maximum. Then put her in her crate. From this point develop a schedule suited to the type and age and habits of the pup. If very young, take her out at least every couple of hours. Observe and learn when she is most likely to relieve herself (When first awake? Right after breakfast? After dinner?). The reason, obviously, is to give her the best chance to do right, and get praise, and thereby learn the routine. When she relieves herself at the appropriate place, give her lots of praise and let her stay out for a bit. If she both poops and pees, even more praise and a longer period of freedom. If she does neither, put her immediately back in the crate and try again in thirty minutes. The concept you are implanting is that every time she does what she's supposed to, *where* she's supposed to, she gets praise and a bit of freedom. Over time, when you're certain she's getting it, the length of time she gets to stay out of the crate gets extended. And ultimately, of course, she gets to stay out the entire day… except when she *wants* to go into her crate. Which she will, because it has become her home. Her own little nest. She will always feel secure there. Of our five, two of them spend a lot of their free time in their crate. The other three are mixed, one choosing not to at all, but none have a problem going in when we have to leave for a while. "Crate yourselves," is the standing command, and five dogs head for three crates.

Yay! Nap time!

At night, of course, the time in the crate is stretched. You will have to judge if your pup can make it all the way through the night. A very young pup might not, but older puppies usually will if they have had the opportunity to relieve themselves just before bedtime and are taken out immediately in the morning. If there's any accident in the crate at night, there is no choice but to wake up and take her out during the night for a few weeks. The entire learning process will be defeated if she is allowed to think that going in the crate is okay.

The trick is to be consistent and on top of the procedure from the beginning. It can become quite a pain to be regular and on time. And it's very easy, especially with a cute puppy, to convince yourself that letting her stay out for an extra hour won't hurt anything. Especially when she's hollering her head off in the crate. But don't do it! Be persistent and consistent. It should take no more than three to four weeks for your pup to have it completely down pat. Two of our five had it in a week. If there's ever any backsliding, just return to the program. Longer in the crate, less time out. There are lots of other sound ways to house-break a pup, but over many years I've found this to be the surest, easiest, least stressful way to do it, with the built-in advantage that whenever your dog needs to be in the crate -- when you're traveling, especially flying, or going to the vet, or just when you're away from the house -- your dog will accept the crate willingly (often happily). We have a soft-shoulder-bag-of-a-crate for Benji when we fly. She gets very excited anytime it comes out. She *knows* that we're off on an adventure. The minute I unzip the front, she crawls in. Once on the plane, she goes under the seat ahead of me and usually I unzip the front so she can see me. Only once has she even thought about crawling out of the bag. But that's Benji. She is the most intuitive dog we've ever owned.

LESSON TWO: GIMME FIVE!

If your pet hasn't fully mastered Lesson One, please go back and finish that lesson before going forward. Don't get into the "cute" stuff until you've mastered control.

WHERE IS MY FOOT?

People generally like for their dog to shake hands. It's a nice way to greet new friends. It promotes interaction. And it's cute. That's where most dog parents stop. But the act of presenting her foot is one of the most important things Benji learns... not *just* to shake hands... but to gain an understanding of what her foot is and the many ways it can be used to extend her knowledge and vocabulary. So, when training Benji, the original command and behavior is always associated with the word *foot*.

"Give me your foot... your foot... your foot."

Not: "Shake hands"... or "Gimme five." Because we want her to understand the concept of *foot*, and other concepts related to her foot that will soon follow. We want her to know what the word really means.

Then, once the behavior is learned (which is basically a hand shake), you can take your dog to new heights with the addition to her vocabulary. She can be easily trained to put her foot on a door... or an object on the floor... or a chair... or even on a light switch… or both feet up on a wall, or chair.

Getting the picture?

Then she can be taught to *dig* with her foot... which can be turned into scratching on a door or a window with her foot... or opening a present with her foot... or doing anything you can think of with her foot, because she now knows what her foot is.

"YOUR FOOT"

Have your dog sit. Stand over her with a treat in your left hand (you no longer need the leash or you should retreat immediately to Lesson One). Hold your right hand out-stretched, palm up (the hand signal), an inch or two in front of your dog's left front paw (the one on your right) and say, "Your foot. Give me your foot." As you say this, and perform the hand signal, touch the top of her foot, near a toenail, with the flat side of the nail of your middle finger. Apply a very slight amount of pressure... and she will move her foot out of the way. If she simply holds it up (as some dogs will), take her foot gently in your hand and rub it or shake it slightly, repeating, "Your foot... your foot..." following immediately with praise, "Good girl! What a good girl you are!" And give her the treat as you praise her.

Then, immediately repeat the process. Over and over. Eight or ten times. Then, give her a rest.

If, in the initial attempt, your pup simply moves her foot over... and puts it back on the floor... then repeat without praise or treat... applying light pressure to the top of her foot with the nail-side of your middle finger. She'll move it again... and, if she once more replaces it on the floor before you can take it in your hand, repeat the process again. Eventually, she will simply hold her foot up so you cannot do that again (rational thinking?)... and then you take it gently in your hand and give her much praise, and the treat. And then do it again and again.

It's very important to remember that the top of the foot is a very sensitive area on most dogs and the pressure you apply should be very slight... just enough to be annoying... not ever enough to be truly uncomfortable or hurt the pup. Heavy pressure is simply not necessary. Your dog will anticipate and move her foot readily.

Very soon, all you'll need to do is say, "Your foot," and offer her your hand (which, again, is the signal)... and before you ever get to touch her, the foot will be in the air... and because you always take the foot in your hand before you praise her and give her a treat, very soon she will simply place her foot in your hand. As she learns to do this, begin to raise your hand a bit higher each time... higher and higher, forcing her to raise her foot higher and higher... until it is very close to her face. You'll see the reason for this later.

If all you want out of it is a handshake, then you're almost there. Using the same hand signal, you can slowly begin to change the verbal cue to "Shake hands" or whatever you like. We had an Australian Terrier, Sydney, who very quickly converted to a "Gimme Five" slap... first one foot, then the other... but her sister, Pepper, didn't have as much spirit and was much too wimpy about it all to get a good hand/paw slap out of her. But the notion of using both feet brings up the next training point...

"OTHER"

Now you have the opportunity to truly expand your dog's vocabulary and comprehension. By teaching her to lift the *other* foot... and by teaching her to do that no matter which foot you ask for first you are teaching her the concept of *other*. And, once learned, that concept can be applied to any *other* behavior.

"Go to the chair. No, the *other* chair."

"Pick up that ball. No, the *other* ball."

"Nudge that bowl. No the *other* bowl."

And before long you have taught your dog to think conceptually. Can you imagine how much easier it is to communicate with a pet who has a vocabulary and can actually think? But I'm getting ahead of myself.

To teach your dog to lift her *other* foot, here's all you have to do. Once she has gotten the "foot" command down pat... once she does it *every* time you ask... even does it without the verbal cue... then, after she has presented her foot, do not give her the praise and treat... but switch hands with the treat... and reverse the above procedure... using your *left* hand by her right paw while saying, "Other foot... other foot." Put emphasis on the word *other*. She already knows what "foot" means... now we're training her to understand what "other" means. Some dogs will pick it up immediately, without you ever having to touch her "other" foot. Some will take longer. Either way, when she lifts that other foot, always take it gently in your hand, just as you did before. Then praise her and pay her with a treat.

Now... as soon as she is offering the "other" foot on command... begin to ask for that foot with your original (right) hand. By switching hands to train her, you were demonstrating visually what "other" means. But now, you want the *word*, the *concept*, not the visual, to lock into her brain... so begin to ask for the "other" foot with your right hand. In *other* words, ask for both feet with the same hand. Sometimes you might have to touch her "other" foot again, but not usually. Benji #3 nailed that change in about ten seconds. Our Yorkie did too. Pepper took longer.

NOW BACK AWAY

Once your dog is offering both feet, and is doing it every time... "Give me your foot... good... now, your other foot... good girl!"... then, and only then... take a couple of steps backward and do the entire routine from there... doing the hand signal but this time not actually taking the foot in your hand, and praising her when she lifts it. Foot and *other* foot. Don't let her be lazy and barely lift it. Keep it high, even if you have to sneak back in and giver her a target with your hand, saying, "Up...up." (Teaching her yet another concept... that "up" means higher). Keep backing further and further away, going over and over the routine, with verbal and hand cues... and if you're diligent, you'll soon be able to do it from several yards away. And, if you've kept her foot high all along, notice how much it looks like a *salute*.

If you like that, and want to put it into your dog's repertoire, all you need to do is slowly add that word to the command and hand signal you already have.

"Your foot. Salute with your foot. Your foot."

Then, after a while, it becomes: "Salute. Use your foot. Salute."

And before long, simply: "Salute."

The reason to use the term "Use your foot" anytime you can is that you will soon be teaching your pup to use her foot to do all sorts of things, so it's good for her to become familiar with the phrase.

26

As you can surely see by now, this process of teaching your dog is not all that different from teaching a very young child. The more you link phrases, the more you teach concepts, the more you build vocabulary... the more you can turn those words into sentences and even sentences into paragraphs. I watched Frank Inn, Benji's original trainer, for years and years, intrigued by his belief that dogs can think, that they can be rational, that they can understand concepts, and if you expect that of them, they won't let you down. If all you expect is a rote response to a command, like Pavlov, that's all you'll get. But when you give your dog the tools, understanding and vocabulary, and lots of love as a reason to please you, you will be surprised at how far they'll reach.

Many times I have played a game when we were in a room full of press to prove this point. With no preparation on Frank's part, in a strange hotel suite, with a room full of strange people, I would do something like this: I might get everyone's attention, pull out a room key and toss it on the floor, then turn to Frank and say, "Okay, Frank... ask Benji to walk over and pick up that room key... take it to Fred over there on the left, put his feet up on the chair... but when Fred reaches for the key, pull away and go over to Bill there in the middle and give him the key... then go over to the right and jump up in Nancy's lap and give her a kiss... then jump down and go back to Bill, take the key from him and bring it back to me. Oh... and do it all by only talking to Benji. Don't ever leave your chair."

Sound impossible? Never, not once, did he fail. Of course I never asked for anything that I didn't think Benji and Frank could pull off... but the point is that he could do that entire routine, exactly as I laid it out, without any rehearsal, sitting in a chair, doing nothing but talking to Benji. Believe me, that kind of communication ability is worth its weight in gold out on a movie set.

Now, the important thing is: once your dog can do all that we've talked about so far, keep working on all of it regularly. Dogs are just like us. If we don't do most things over and over, we forget. Don't let her forget.

DID YOU KNOW...

Which of the following is true?

When calling a dog who is reluctant to come to you, the best thing to do is to:

1. Chase him.

2. Stand your ground and keep calling him firmly until he comes.

3. Sit quietly and ignore him until he comes to you on his own.

4. Lie down on the ground, or squat, getting your head as close to his eye-level as possible, and call him.

5. Offer him food.

When your pup is reluctant to come to you, it usually means one of two things. Either he has done something he knows he shouldn't have done. Or you've frightened him in some way, perhaps by yelling or talking harshly to him. Or both. For example: you caught him in the act of chewing on a chair and bellowed like banshee! He takes off like a shot, and you wonder why he's not obeying your command to come. It's because he's no dummy. He knows that tone of voice, and most likely knows he was doing something he shouldn't be doing. So he's not about to come willingly to this screeching giant towering over him to receive what at best might be a scolding and a period of time-out in the crate. So all the screaming and hollering you can muster will only make him more certain that this is not a perfect time to be close to you. Obviously, chasing him is not the right answer, even though it seems too often to be our first response. In open spaces, you will never catch him. And even if there's an outside chance you might catch him because he's in confined quarters, it's still not the right answer. You will only scare him to death and perhaps leave a lasting memory that will re-up every time he looks at you. Or with some dogs, puppies especially, he might decide it's a game, and that's the last thing you want. You want your dog to come to you *any*time you feel it's necessary. *Any* time. His safety could depend upon it. Say, for example, he's gotten out and is headed for traffic in the street. You screech at him to come back, which only scares him. The last thing you want to do is drive him away from you by screaming or chasing him right into traffic. And, at a moment like this, food will have little or no effect. He's needs to feel immediately safe. He needs to believe that you are the best solution to his immediate emotional problem.

The correct answer for re-acquiring your pet is Number 4. Be a dog. Be a friend. Get down to his level. Drop to one knee. If he's still reluctant, get lower. And call to him. Sweetly, but firmly. Calmly. As quickly as possible if safety is an issue. The very fact that you've dropped to his level is not ordinary. That will usually stop him in his tracks, if for no other reason than to digest this weirdness. And the shorter, smaller, less fearsome image -- one much closer to his own size, as opposed to one towering over him -- will immediately make him feel more comfortable with the "you" option. As silly as this sounds, it works! I've never seen it fail. And there's an added benefit. It points out to you in spades that, at the moment, your dog is afraid of you, and you need to compromise to remove that fear. Also, dropping to the ground tends to deflate your anger (and ego). How can you stay angry when you're down on your knees or lying on your belly gushing, "Chum here poochie woochie baby girl."

But… once he decides he will trust this lowered, smaller, compromising, sweetened you, be absolutely certain you don't betray that trust when he comes to you, or it'll never work again. If you feel you must go on record with some sort of admonition for bad deeds done, then wait a bit. The moment has passed anyway while you were chasing him all over the yard. So praise him softly for coming. Not gushy. Just comfort him a bit. Then take him calmly to the infraction, make sure he sees it, and put him calmly in his crate for a while saying something like my Dad used to say to me, "This hurts me more than it hurts you." I never really believed him but in later years I've at least come to appreciate the effort. Perhaps your pup will too.

Above all, while working on other commands, work diligently on the "Come" command. Most people don't (even I'm guilty) because your dogs so naturally want to come to you, you tend to think you don't need to work on that one. But the difference between Benji and some of our other dogs points up the need. Because I have worked with Benji in sessions on the *come* command, and praised her and given her treats for coming, it has become as ingrained as any of her other vocabulary. When the front door is open, and the UPS truck pulls up the driveway, every dog in the house races out yapping. I can stop Benji in her tracks with one "Benji, come!" If I'm quick enough, I can stop Shaggy with two or three *comes*. But not so with the others. They haven't had the mileage on that word so it's not a priority. I've never made it a priority, so they don't. But it is really valuable, especially in dangerous or emergency situations, to be able to stop your pet on a dime.

LESSON THREE: BELLY DOWN

WHY LIE DOWN?

In movie-making, of course, there are numerous times when we need Benji to lie down. But there are other good reasons to accomplish this one early on. First, it's a natural follow up to "Sit" and "Stay". "Sit" and "Stay" are good "control" commands when you want your pup to be out of the action. "Lie Down" is even better. When a dog is sitting, he's still ready to pounce, run, leap, and play. But there's an extra barrier drawn psychologically when a dog is lying down. It's more of a "calm down" position. And a variation on this theme produced one of the simplest yet most appreciated actions that Benji does when performing in public. More on that in a bit. The first two things we'll learn are "Lie Down" and "Put your Head Down."

"LIE DOWN"

Now that your pup is getting the picture that commands and hand signals are associated with desired actions, praise and treats, he should be anxious for more. You'll need the leash again for this one. And a treat in one hand. Attach the leash and ask your dog to *sit*. The new command, of course, is "Lie Down." The hand signal is a downward motion of the same hand that holds the treat, open palm downward (once he has seen the treat, you can wedge it in the joint between your thumb and forefinger so you can still work with an open palm down). In the beginning, the motion should be very large, starting well above the dog's head, swooping all the way down to

32

where the flat of your palm actually touches the floor or ground. Put a bit of emphasis on the word *"Down"* just as you make the downward motion with your hand. This helps your dog visually associate the word "down" with a movement *down...* and this will help later with commands like "Get down." As with learning the conceptual command "other," learning the conceptual difference between up and down is important to vocabulary and communication.

When you say the command and make the downward motion, no doubt your dog will watch your hand (it has a treat in it, right?), often curiously, figuring you're trying to communicate *some*thing, but he doesn't know exactly what. That's where the leash comes in. At the same time you issue the command and do the hand signal, gently tug downward on the leash. This puts pressure on the back of his neck, the strong part, so it won't hurt him. *Do not jerk on the leash!* Just apply firm downward pressure. That will usually do it. Enough to make him uncomfortable sitting... and, being no dummy, he does the natural thing. He lies down. Explode with praise, pats, hugs... and a treat. Then have him sit and do it again. And again. And again and again. Then take a break.

If the downward pressure of the leash does *not* cause him to lie down, or if he's such a big dog that he's stronger than you, here are two tricks that almost always work. First try this: When you make the downward motion with your hand, drop to one knee and lower your chin until it actually touches the ground (or for us older folk, *almost* touches the ground). He will immediately want to get to your level. Here's one of his rare opportunities to lick you in the face!! Can't pass that up! It makes a game out of it... but as soon as he's dropped to the deck, praise him, hug him, and give him that treat. Then do it again and again. Then take a break.

As I write this, we have a new five-month-old German Shepherd and it took him only ten or fifteen minutes to get this. He will, of course, need lots of reinforcement, but he's got the concept. But if it's still not working for you (almost always does), the trick to add to the mix is to make your downward tug on the leash just a bit off to one side so that the angle puts him a bit off balance. Rather than risk falling, he'll lie down. In rare circumstances, I've had to help a dog "get it" with my hands, actually pulling a foot one way while nudging the body the other way. Again, this causes an uncomfortable fear of losing his balance (plus, he doesn't like you messing with his legs) so he'll usually lie down. I prefer getting him to more or less lie down on his own (for example to get that lick in the face) because when he does it on his own, he'll remember it better; and the concept will stick faster.

In any case, once you have him lying down, and you've repeated it several times, each time with lavish praise and treats, he will very quickly get the concept. Those words and that motion mean *lie down… and then I get praise and a treat!* Several of our dogs needed none of the extra tricks. Just the downward motion and their own logic worked. Work with him until he *really* has it and you can effect a lie down from a few feet away… *without* squatting or dropping to one knee. Only then move on to:

"HEAD DOWN"

There are only two good reasons I can think of for training a "Head Down." One: In a film, when you want to portray a dog sleeping you have to start *some*where and…Two: It's cute. Almost always gets an "Awwwww" when performing in public. The method is merely an extension of what you've just done in the section above. Same motion, just smaller. Same tricks. Different command.

Once you have your dog lying down on command, each time, every time… and staying in place, then reach for another treat and tell her "Head Down," the downward motion right in front of her nose until your hand is flat on the ground, just far enough away from her nose that she cannot get to the treat until you want her to. Again, you can use a downward tug the leash if necessary, but it usually isn't because the pup now understands the "down" concept… and there's only one thing left to go down… her head. Plus she wants to get as low as that treat! Making her stay in that position can be a bit harder, but you have the "stay" command well implanted, right?

One of our dogs actually went all the way right from the start. On the "Lie Down" command she would lie down *and* put her head down. I actually had to back her up and break it into two parts by holding the treat a little higher on the first command, then all the way down on the second command. Why ever, would I do that? As I said before, having your dog "lie down" is not an unexpected piece of training, but the when you "top it" with that ever-cute drop of the head to the floor, and those big eyes looking up at you, your audience will melt. Once your dog has it mastered, you'll see what I mean. Which brings us to the extension I mentioned earlier:

"ON YOUR SIDE"

Once your pup has the "lie down" mastered, usually a roll over her head with your "treat" hand, accompanied by the command: *On Your Side*, will cause her to roll over on her side. The reasoning is that she will try to follow your hand with the treat in it, and when you roll it over the top of her head she can no longer see it unless she rolls over on to her side. Again… *logic*. What will logically cause her to do the desired action? If, for some reason that *doesn't* happen, usually a little nudge with your other hand, or a tug on her collar, will show her what you want. And, again, repeat it over and over until you can do the whole thing, including the little "roll-over" hand motion, from a standing position. Always give her the treat while she is on her side, not after she gets up. This will help her understand the concept. Then, if she doesn't automatically put her head down on the floor when she rolls on to her side, reinforce this with the same "head down" lesson used above after the "lie down."

Now… this is where the fun comes in. Your audience is already impressed that you can cause your pup to lie down… put her head down… then roll over on her side… and again put her head down. Now, you will teach her to stay – on her side, with her head down -- while you simply walk away. I have no idea why this impresses folks so, but it does. The fact is, if you teach this softly and firmly using the techniques described in the "Sit and Stay" section above, it's very simply done, because, frankly, for all but the wildest puppies, this is a very comfortable, highly regarded position. So getting her to stay is usually quite acceptable.

Then, what I do, after I walk fifteen or twenty feet away, saying "Stay" all the while, is stop and peek back over my shoulder as if to see if she's still on her side. Usually when I peek back, Benji wags her tail. The audience laughs. I say, "No tail!" Sharply. And regardless of what she does the audience laughs again. I have made no attempt to train her to *not* wag her tail… because it's actually funnier if she does. Then I turn to the audience and say something like "Just can't teach her anything,"… and that gets another laugh. If perchance she *does* stop wagging her tail, I just turn and smile, as if to say, *isn't this simply the smartest dog you've ever seen.* My guess is that Benji knows exactly what's going on, and knows this is her moment to one-up me.

In any case, when we're done with any action that requires a *stay*, I always happily say "Okay!!" And Benji pops up and comes for her treat. And that quick popping up is, in itself, an action that we use in the movies… for example, when she's frustrated over something, then suddenly has an idea! A *good* idea! We might have her lie down and drop her head down on the deck in frustration… then suddenly pop up with an alert look… and in the right context, that quick action after the slow, moping frustration, always reads like a light bulb! Sudden idea!

We've covered a lot of ground quickly in this section, but the thing to remember is to take each new action, one at a time, and train it in slowly and with repetition. And do *not* go on to the next action until the current one is thoroughly learned by your pup. Too much too quick can become a jumble in anyone's mind. Also remember, different dogs learn at different paces. Benji #3 is a very quick study. Among a myriad of other traits, that's one of the reasons she was selected to be Benji. And we spent more than three months searching the shelters of the country for just the right face with just the right temperament, and just the right brain. There are lots of other dogs who will learn as quickly as she does. And lots who will not. So be patient and work at your dog's pace, and you'll both be very pleased with the result.

"No!"

As I've mentioned, we have five dogs. They all know the meaning of the word "No." None have been formally trained to know that. It has all come from usage. From the first day your dog is in your house, you will be admonishing your pup for inappropriate behavior. The first trick is to only use *one* word. Just one. And, of course, the word is "No!" Knowing this, it's amazing how our family of Kathleen, three kids and myself, all tend, in the heat of battle, to let fly whatever comes to mind at the moment.

"Stop it!"

"Don't do that!"

"Put that down!"

"Quit that!"

"Get outta there!"

"Leave that alone!"

And on and on. Way too many phrases. The simple key to teaching your pup the meaning on *no* is to always and only (at least in the beginning) use the word "No!" With an exclamation! Said sharply. Maybe with a whack of your hand against your leg (for noise only!) or a whack of a folded newspaper against your hand. Your dog isn't stupid. Your tone of voice…. and perhaps a loud noise says loud and clear that you don't like what he's doing. Very soon, if you can make yourself – and your family – only use the word *no*, you will no longer need the loud noise, the exclamation point, or the harsh voice. Because your pup will fully understand the meaning of the word. Our five-month old Shepherd has it already. A simple, quiet, calm "No" will stop him in his tracks, whatever he's doing. He also knows "Leave it"… "Out"… "Down"… and "Outside." All learned the same way, merely through usage. With praise when he responds correctly. And all the words, now, are available without the exclamation point. But, in the beginning, take just one word at a time until your pup fully understands it. Then start adding others, also one at a time. And watch the comprehension grow!

Do the same with positive words. In the beginning, say only "Good boy!" when you're praising him. Or whatever phrase you like, just be consistent. Stick to one phrase. And say it with joy and smiles. Be gushy. Before long, you can tone back the gushiness and he'll still get it, and be happy to get it. When you use too many phrases, even though your tone of voice gives him the praise, he's not building his vocabulary. At this writing, with Chewie the young Shepherd, a simple, casual, off-hand "Good boy" tells him that he's on the right track. No big deal. No gush. Just a way to say "Cool. Keep on keepin' on."

"COME"

For our family of dogs, the word "Come" became a part of their vocabulary through usage, just like the words above. But once your pup understands "sit" and "stay," you can reinforce the word "come" by walking away saying "Stay…stay…" then turn, with treat in hand, and say "Come." Give her the treat and do it again. Your dog will consider this one a no-brainer and will have it down in a matter of moments. And, as mentioned earlier, mileage on this command will be well worth   it.

LESSON FOUR: OFF YOUR BOOTY

"ON YOUR FEET"

Now that your dog has learned to sit, and lie down, and lie on her side, it's time to get her back on her feet. This will be your first lesson in logical, creative (meaning trial-and-error) training. Three of our dogs have this vocabulary and all three learned it very quickly; but all three learned it completely differently. What worked for one did not work for the others. And, as I said in the beginning, the real reason for this book is to train *you* to be logical and to figure it out as you go along. Good dog training is logic and love. And, of course, repetition and persistence. That's it.

Chewie, our Shepherd puppy, learned it this way. With your pup on a "sit" and "stay," drop your hand to your side, palm toward your dog, and flip your fingers several times as if you were closing your fist (what your hand signal is really saying is "Up with your booty."). At the same time say, "On your feet." As you're doing this, reach out with your foot and touch one of your pup's back toenails. Just touch it. Don't press hard. Do not hurt the pup. It's much the same as when you were teaching "Your foot." Just enough touch to make her uncomfortable. The dog's natural reaction to this (*most* dogs) is to move her foot out of harm's way… and to do this (usually) she must stand up. Yes! Praise her a bunch and give her a treat. And do it again. And again. Very quickly, she'll get the idea that if she stands up *before* you touch her foot, you stop, you praise, and you give her a treat. Very soon, just the slightest movement in her direction, while giving the hand signal and saying "On your feet" will result in your dog standing. And soon after that, you won't even need to make the forward move. It took Chewie less than ten minutes to figure all this out. Of course, we still needed repetition to set the vocabulary and make it stick, but he "got it" very quickly.

But… it didn't work quite that way with Sydney, one of our Australian Terriers. She would immediately stand, but the minute I withdrew, before I could praise her, she would sit right back down. So I tried a couple of things. When I tell Sydney to sit, she likes to walk right up close to me. Remember, that's the way she learned it. Having to look up at the figure towering over her. So the minute she got *on her feet* I took a step backward to see if that would cause her to follow with a step, thus staying on her feet long enough to get some praise. And she did exactly that – took a step forward toward me – and then sat right back down again. Hmmm… I thought. Well, let's go straight to the obvious and see how a bright dog deals with it. I gave the signal, said "On your feet," and reached over her and lifted her haunches into a standing position… and said "Stay."

She did… and I praised… gave her a treat… then started over, telling her to sit. I had to do that maybe four times before she totally "got it"… and from that point on, the hand signal and verbal command were all it took. This probably wouldn't have worked if it were the first command I ever taught her, but by now she understands that what we're trying to do here is develop ways to communicate. "See!" I say to the naysayers who don't believe dogs can think rationally. All you need do is ask. From that point on, it was merely some repetition for practice to set the vocabulary and Sydo had it.

But… Benji, the brightest one of the pack, responded yet a different way. Touching her toenail did no good whatsoever. Maybe she's too smart. When I would touch her rear toenail with my foot, she would merely scooch away from the touch on her butt. Didn't matter which side. The result was the same. So, remembering the experience with Sydney, I gave up on the foot-touch altogether and resorted to the "haunch lift," giving her the signal and command as I

41

leaned down to lift her haunches and drop them back into a standing position. "Oh," she said. "I get it. No problem." It took maybe three times doing that before she began to take the command immediately and stand up. Amazing, say I. Even I wouldn't have bet good money that she would get it from that bit of un-natural action, especially so quickly. Oh me of little faith!

So, one of the above patterns will most likely work with your dog, but if you have to get creative, remember, you know your dog better than anybody. I once knew a dog who would leap to his feet anytime anyone said the words *ice cream*. With that dog, those words might be the place to start. Get the picture? If something isn't working within a reasonable amount of time, don't keep doing it over and over. Instead, do a little creative thinking about what might work with your dog, and give it a try. There are no hard and fast rules, and only *you* are the expert with *your* dog. All you're trying to do is establish good communication with your pup. Whatever gets you there is the tool to use.

Once you have your dog standing on cue, here's a cute expansion of the theme with results that will bring peals of laughter from friends and family. Don't do this until "On your feet" is an automatic part of your pup's vocabulary, but once it is… try this: the moment he stands, say "Good!" and take a step or two toward him with your hand in the same position, palm toward the dog, like the stay command, but moving your hand as if you were pushing the dog backwards (or building a sand pile)… and say "Back, back, back, back!" As you crowd toward him, he will instinctively take a step backward, then another, and another. You say "Good!! Good!!" And give him a treat. Then walk back up to your original position, calling him as you go. "Good, come on. Come" Then once he's back to his original position, go again, stepping right toward the dog, saying "Back, back, back, back!" And so forth. With Benji this becomes a game that she loves to play. Back and forth, like an accordion. And for some reason audiences laugh themselves silly at it. Maybe because Benji's having so much fun with it.

And her understanding of the command is not without use on a movie set. For example, to get just *one* backward step, like a step backward in fear, as if someone had just stepped into the room with a big rifle… the desired reaction will come from the hand signal just once or twice with a "Back, back…STAY!"

HAVE YOU EVER NOTICED?

Have you ever noticed how your dog reflects, your moods, your anxiety, your stress, your intensity? I've never met one who doesn't. Knowing this, and paying attention to it, is very good for your dog's health and well-being, and it can be a useful tool. If you give your dog a command and you're all bubbly and gushy and bouncy, your dog will be the same. As in the "Back, back, back" command above. When performing for an audience, I always do it happily, making it a fun game. And Benji responds in kind. But in the second example, when all I want is a single step backward and a hard intensive look, that's the way I give the command. No happiness in the voice or demeanor at all. None. Minimal stiff hand signal. Almost harsh in the verbal command. And a sudden, unexpected, loud **"Stay!"** issued even before the first step is fully completed, making it seem not only fearful, but unsure. Like *Oh my, what do I do now?* You try it. You'll see exactly what I'm talking about. Sometimes I do it both ways for an audience when I might be speaking about how Benji works on a movie set. The two performances seem starkly different, but they both emerge right out of an understanding of that one word of vocabulary.

Now try this: say it very softly, with almost no hand movement at all. Chances are your dog will take an itty bitty step backward. Surprising? Why? If I did the same to you, that's how you'd respond. Why shouldn't your dog? My first encounter with understanding that a dog could and would utilize emotion as a learned response came while making the first Benji movie. In the scene, Benji needed to mope down an alley looking as if he'd lost his last friend. Frank was yelling at the top of his voice, "Shame on you!!! Get that head down!! Shame on you!!" It broke my heart and I pulled Frank off into a corner and said we would have to find another way to do this. Frank erupted in laughter and said that obviously I didn't understand dogs as well as he thought I did. He called Benji over (who by the way was happy as a lark after just being yelled at) and screeched the same commands at him. Benji's head dropped and he seemed to be consumed with sadness… but the minute Frank said (happily) "Okay. Good kid!" the sadness was gone. Instantly! And he was as happy as could be. He *understood* that when Frank bellowed "Shame on you!" he was supposed to look sad. Perhaps the first time it ever happened Benji might have thought for a moment that he was being shamed… until Frank praised him and gave him a treat! Then he understood. Because he understands the *process* of learning and communication. *Show me. Praise me. Then, leave me alone. I've got it. Don't be a bore.* The moral, don't ever underestimate your pup.

Another thing Frank would do that's a lot of fun and you might try yourself is to take out three treats that are exactly the same. Frank would ask two people to touch one treat each and remember which one they touched. Then he would tell everybody watching that, for health reasons, Benji was trained to never eat food that anyone has touched. And sure enough, he would offer each one that had been touched to a hungry Benji, but Benji wouldn't eat. Then when he offered the untouched treat, Benji would, of course, gobble it up.

The canine star, of course, didn't give a whit whether anyone had touched a treat. And he had no clue which ones had been touched. But he and Frank had a silent, undetectable communication going on. It was based entirely on tension. Even though Frank's smile looked perfectly genuine, and his hand motion offering the treat looked very natural, when he didn't want Benji to eat, he would emanate tension out of every pour in his body… in effect silently saying to Benji with all the tenseness he could muster, *Don't you dare touch that treat or you'll spend the rest of your life in the crate!* It took me months to figure it out but one day when Frank was out of the room, I tried it, and it worked perfectly. A big praise for Benji and a big smile for me! Now Benji #3 is doing it as well. Try it. You'll be amazed at what you can communicate to your pup without uttering a word. The first few times you might need to be a bit more obvious than you will be in final performance but soon you and your dog will be amazing your friends. And remember, as with all training, immediately praise your pup and give him a treat when he does it right. The first time he might think you're being scary but the minute you praise him and give him a treat, he'll understand that it's just a desired response. That's the beauty of training this way. Practice with the tension, and *every* time your dog refuses the treat, relax and praise him and let him have it. Very quickly, he'll see the point and you both will have fun with this new private communication.

LESSON FIVE: NOW FIGURE IT OUT

If you and your dog have come this far, you're way ahead of most dog owners. And hopefully much happier companions for all you've learned. From here, the exercises will get shorter because your dog learns more quickly now and you already know that you must praise, and pay, and repeat each exercise until your pup has added it to his vocabulary.

Also, I will be setting up the objective of the exercise, then asking you to stop and think about how you would approach it before I tell you how I approached it. You and your pup understand the drill now and very soon the rest will be up to the two of you.

"NUDGE IT"

The objective: to train your dog to *nudge* an object with her nose... like nudging a ball or toy across the floor... or nudging a switch to flip on a light. It's probably not a particularly useful command for you, but you and your pup can have a lot of fun with it. For us, when filming a movie, we couldn't do without it. In the original *Benji*, Benji "nudged" an open pudding cup to his new-found girlfriend Tiffany. He also "nudged" Tiffany herself in a show of affection. He "nudged" a popcorn bag held by his police officer friend; and a crumpled piece of paper on the floor which triggered the idea of how to save his friends. In *Benji the Hunted*, he did a lot of "nudging" of cougar cubs and bits of food. In *Oh Heavenly Dog* he "nudged" a phone off the hook, papers on a desk, pottery, and windows. In *Benji Off the Leash* it was a latch on a dog's cage, and a gate, and a turkey leg, and his mom. Hardly a shooting day goes by that doesn't need a "nudge" of *some* sort.

So how would you start? What's the first "nudge" you would attempt to train. Think about it for a moment. What does your dog "nudge" naturally. Or what *could* he "nudge" naturally. Come up with your own ideas before you read on. My suggestions begin on the next page.

When I begin to work on the "nudge it" command, I want the quickest, easiest way to get the point across… to get the command firmly into my dog's vocabulary… and there is a natural "nudge" they all have in common. We have crate-trained all our dogs. When we leave for a period, they all stay in their crates. And when we return, I do no more than unlatch the doors to the crates. The dogs take it from there. Each one opens her own door and comes out on her own. A natural nudge until the door swings open.

So that's where I would begin when working on the nudge. Put the dog in the crate. Shut the door, but don't latch it. Tell the dog to stay. Withdraw a treat. Let him see it. Then say "Come. Nudge it. Nudge it with your nose." And praise and pay with a treat when he does. Then do it again… and again… and again. Once I feel he has the concept, I would move it to a totally different but similar object, like a door in the house. Put the dog on one side, you on the other, with a treat of course. Have your dog sit and stay. Close the door almost all the way but not quite, and repeat the drill as done in the crate. Doggie doors would work. Screen doors. Even a floor cabinet or pantry door. Do not let your pup use his foot to open the door. Say "No" and do not give him a treat if he does. He only gets the praise and the treat if he nudges with his nose. That's important. He must associate the use of his head and nose with the command "Nudge it. Nudge it with your nose."

Once he has the concept well implanted, I would move to a similarly moving item, but more of an object… like a hardback book. Lay the book on the floor and prop open the front cover to almost ninety degrees. Point to it and repeat the same command. It might take him a minute to make the transition, but most usually will. He doesn't have to nudge it much for it to flop open… and receive dollops of praise and a treat. Do it again and again… then prop the front cover open at about forty-five degrees. He'll have to do more work to get this one to flop open, but once accomplished, he'll definitely have the concept locked in. Then transfer it to a ball... a toy... a glass... whatever.

If you don't have a crate to start with, you might try hanging a piece of cardboard on string from a stick, and have your dog nudge through it... or cut a door in a large cardboard box. If you have a big dog, even the front door of your house would work. I've used a big beach ball, confining the dog in an area that forces him to nudge the beach ball to get out and get to the treat.

"Use Your Foot!"

Now we get back to the use of "Your foot." And to expanding your pups ability to not only understand words, but phrases and even sentences. Now that he knows what his foot is, and knows how to offer a foot and the *other* foot, we will teach him to actually use a foot to accomplish a task. Let's say, for example, that you want to teach your pup to scratch on a door. What would you do first? How would you approach it. Remember, the key is to begin with something your dog will or could do naturally. Spend a moment thinking this through before you read on. My suggestions begin on the next page.

Also remember that my suggestions are just that. *Suggestions.* You might've come up with the perfect solution. What we're trying to do here is not lay down rules for training, but rather explore the thinking process that will enable you to train just about anything you want to train.

What I would do first with this one is to identify something my dog loves to play with. A toy or a bone or a stick. If it happens to be a dog that doesn't play with toys much, I'd use a treat. In this case definitely a dry treat. Put your dog on a sit and stay and let him watch you bury the toy just under the surface of the ground (or preferably sand). Then call him over and say "Use your foot! Dig it up! Use your foot! Dig it up. Go on! Dig it up! Use your foot!"

The reason for using both phrases is that one states the tool (foot) and the other asks for action (dig). And both will be used in a different context soon. Your dog will come and in all likelihood dig up the toy. It must be deep enough that he cannot just "nudge" a bit of dirt away and grab it with his mouth. That's why sand is good. He will dig because it's a very natural action to dig for something he wants. When he retrieves the toy… as usual, lots of praise and a treat. And repetition. Until it's on cue every time. Then take it to the next venue. Like the door. Your dog now understands the meaning of "Dig it up. Use your foot" so you just need to bridge the small gap of transference of that command to another object. So I would go back to the same door where I taught the "nudge it" command. Put your dog on one side and you on the other. Make sure he knows you have a treat. Then begin the process of telling him to "Come. Dig it up. Use your foot." Over and over. What is he likely to do?"

Right. He's going to probably try to nudge his way through. So put your foot, or booty, or whatever against your side of the door so that it will not open, and keep saying, "No. Use your foot, your foot. Dig it up. Use your foot!" And do not let him through until he does, which he ultimately will. If he just paws at it, be sure you allow the door to swing open a little and praise him to keep him working at it. At the right time, let him open it all the way and praise and reward him. Then do it again. And again.

Next, you should be able to transfer this to an object that your pup will *not* pass through… like scratching open a drawer… scratching the phone off the hook… or pawing at a light switch to turn it off (Now he can nudge it *on* and with his foot turn it *off*). Benji has used this education to open a screen door from the outside. To turn a pudding cup over. To open drawers, to move rocks out of his path, to scratch at windows to get people's attention on the other side. And much more. But beware. Now your dog knows how to do all sorts of things that most dogs don't, like go in and out when he wants, raid the pantry, turn on the lights. You might want to keep your car keys hidden.

In the early days, whenever we would do a television or public appearance, Frank used to bring along a rural mailbox, the kind with a red flag on the side, mounted on a Benji-height stand. On command, with a letter in his mouth (Pick it up. Hold it"), Benji would stand on his back legs ("Put your feet up."), then Benji would open the front door of the mailbox ("Your foot, your foot. Dig it up.") put the letter in the mailbox ("Put it in there. Go on. Put it in. Drop it."), "nudge" the door closed and "nudge" the red flag up with his nose.

Now that your pup has full understanding that he can do things with his "foot," you can teach him all sorts of other footed things. Like putting one foot on an object. Or both feet. "Put your feet up"… on a chair, on you, on a wall, on somebody. A secondary benefit to this is that once he learns to put his feet up when you tell him to, he gets the idea much more quickly that's it's not good to put his feet up when he's not told to. That was a "discovered" secondary value of teaching our Shepherd puppy to put his feet up. He's a puppy. He likes to jump up on people. But he's *big!* And even though he understands the meaning of "No" it has to be said *before* he lays somebody flat to save the party being jumped on. After I taught him to put his feet up on command, and kept doing it every so often, and praising him for it, he seemed to get the idea that if it wasn't called for he shouldn't do it. A couple of times I've seen him pause long enough to think about it before jumping on someone. Just long enough for me to say "No" and stop it before it happened.

"PICK IT UP"

What's the easiest way to teach your dog to pick something up?

Right. Start with something he will pick up naturally. Like a favorite toy. Or even a treat, if necessary. All he has to know is that's it's okay, and he'll pick it up. When accompanied by a finger-point to the object, and the command "Pick it up, pick it up," then praise when he does, and a treat, he'll get the picture very quickly. Then you can transfer it to something that isn't a favorite. Point to the object. Issue the verbal command over and over. Then praise him and reward him when he does as you request. Keep saying the command and pointing over and over until he does pick it up. If he doesn't, then go back to the favorite toy and start over. He *will* get it.

"HOLD IT."

If she wants to drop the object before you want her to, use your fingers to gently hold her mouth closed on the object as you say repeatedly: "Hold it." And squeeze just a bit as you say the command. Do this several times, then praise, praise, praise, and giver her a treat. Then over and over again until she fully understands… which shouldn't take long now because she should fully have the picture of what training sessions are all about, and she wants to please.

52

"Drop it."

Have you ever had trouble getting something away from your dog? Make sure he understands the "Drop it" command and you won't have that problem any more. What's the best way to start? Think about it for a moment. When is a dog going to naturally drop something out of his mouth?

Right. When he wants to put something else into it. Like a treat!

Let him pick up his favorite toy. Show him the treat. Up close! Then say "Drop it!" He will, because he wants that treat. Then praise him and give it to him. Do it over and over.

The real mark of how well you set this command is by letting him have a large treat in his mouth and before he's had a chance to chow down, tell him to drop it. That one's tough, but doable if the two of you have done your home work well.

A Note About Your Fingers...

Even though your mother taught you that it's not polite to point, it can become a very good command module for you and your dog. I've been told by folks whose credits indicate they should know better that a dog cannot grasp such a vague, hazy notion as comprehending information transfer by a mere point of a finger. I say, "Watch my dogs." This is probably helped along by the fact that our dogs have learned hand signals along with most (not all) commands, so the "visual" notion is well set. With a couple of my dogs, I can take them all over the house with little more than a finger for pointing and an open palm for stopping and staying. A finger touch upon an object I want them to pick up. A point to the sofa onto which I want them to jump. A point off when it's time to jump down. Maybe emphasized on occasion by a snap of a finger for punctuation. A finger snap will get their attention, and will stop them cold in their tracks when they know it's coming from me. They look. I point. They go. And do. The more you work on all this, the more you will come to believe that your dog can understand pretty much anything you'd like him to. It's up to you and how much time you choose to invest in it.

And Now...

We could go on and on, but if you've come this far, you and your pup should be well equipped for a lifetime of healthy dialog. Just stop and think: *what will cause her to do naturally what I would like to train her to do?* The answer is your key. Additional examples...

"Shake your head."

To teach Benji to shake her head (used often to show frustration in Benji movies), a small tickle inside the ear with a little finger, just enough to disturb the wax in the ear, will usually cause a shake of the head. When accompanied by the command "Shake your head" and a shake of your hand as if your were shaking water from your fingers, and followed by praise and a treat... you have a head shake on command. Then it can be dialed down by making just a very slight motion and whispering... or up by an excited motion and loud command, often getting a full body shake. Benji has come to understand the words "little bitty" and "big"... *little bitty shake...* or ***BIG** shake*. Count the number of times head shakes are used in any Benji movie.

"Sneeze"

Same goes for a *sneeze* on command. Find what will make your dog sneeze on command. It shouldn't need to be said at this stage that you should never do anything that will hurt, or irritate your dog, or endanger her health. In other words, *no pepper!*

I begin by saying the word "Sneeze" every time she sneezes. "Good sneeze," I'll say and give her a pat. This is just to get her familiar with the word. Then when I start actual training, it's a trial and error process. Sometimes a little puff of air into her nose will do it. Or a feather to tickle her nose. Or just a light (very light) squeezing of her nostrils together to tickle the inside. Accompanied by the command "Sneeze" and a downward flick of your hand from your nose to your waist. This works with most dogs, but I have two for whom I've never found the key (admittedly, with five dogs, I tend to do what comes easiest for each and usually don't obsess or commit huge amounts of time on things that don't come easy... except for Benji). The bottom line, if you can discover what causes your dog to sneeze naturally, you can train it on command. Even then, with this one, what I've learned over many dogs is that if the pup cannot generate a real sneeze, some just won't do it. Others, like Chelsea, our Yorkie, will somehow find a real sneeze every time I ask for it. Benji's sneezes usually show up in movies as disgusted snorts. Some tiny, like a sigh. Some very broad. As if saying "Good grief!"

Teaching a sneeze is potentially the most difficult thing we've mentioned yet. But, as I mentioned, Chelsea sneezes every time I ask for it... but, believe it or not, we have one who has never learned to speak. I have never found the trick that links the command and the wave of a fore finger (as if saying *no* to a child) to the actual bark. It's a matter of time commitment, or lack thereof, on my part. Usually the action comes from excitement. Most dogs bark if you get them excited, jump up and down, waving your finger like some sort of mad man, and chirping "Speak, speak, speak!" over and over in an excited voice. But Sydney just gapes at me like I was an idiot. If I would commit the time to the task, Sydney and I could work it out. But, again, I'm not obsessed with it, so I've left it alone, convinced that some day it'll happen naturally. And if not, that's okay too.

Fortunately, it's Sydney, not Benji. Although an interesting thing happened when Benji was first taught Benji to speak. She learned the action just fine, very quickly. She just didn't make a noise. Not a sound. We have no idea why, but I like it the way it. Now when we're on a public appearance and I ask her to speak, she snaps her mouth as if she were speaking, and I turn to the audience and say, "It's easy to teach a dog to speak. What's difficult is teaching her that in the movies we dub the sound in later." The audience always laughs. But, as it turns out, the joke's on me, because, recently, Benji has actually started barking sometimes. So now I'm trying to figure out how to actually train her to do it silently so we don't lose that part of the performance.

AND ON AND ON...

You can teach your dog to yawn on cue, to scratch a flea, to close her eyes... whatever comes to your mind, as long as you start with whatever causes her to do it naturally and you devote the time and patience to develop it slowly and properly. With love and affection. And logic. Now it's up to you... and your pup.

Have fun!

APPENDIX

Benji Facts

Since the search for the Benji #3 began, Benji has generated more than a billion exposures on television, radio, and in newspapers for the adoption efforts of shelters and rescue groups everywhere!

More than 72,000,000 people have watched Benji movies in theaters, over half of them adults.

Three of Benji's movies have grossed within the top 10% of box office grosses for their year of release.

More than one billion people have watched Benji movies and programs on television.

In September of 2002, *People Magazine* placed the movie *Benji* in their Top 20 Best Ever Family Movies.

Two of Benji's primetime specials were nominated for Emmys.

The title theme of the film *Benji* was nominated for an Oscar, and won the Golden Globe Award.

Benji has twice been awarded AGVA's Animal Entertainer of the year award.

Benji has been a frequent visitor to various top ten popularity lists, including Performer Q, and a Young Miss magazine poll ranked Benji #5 among all males.

Benji was the second animal ever to be inducted into the Animal Actors Hall of Fame.

USA Today ranked Benji the Hunted third best among all of the summer's hot movie releases.

Benji Off the Leash won the Genesis Award for the best family film of the year. And is a *Reader's Digest* Family Favorite.

Love, hope, and the value of persistence toward a goal are the heart and soul of every Benji story. Benji is not about special effects, potty humor, flash-cuts, screeching sound, and warlike monsters. It's emotionally involving family entertainment that's happy, sad, and full of suspense, and has become classic around the world with kids and parents alike for the small and simple reason that it just plain makes you feel good.

Benji$_{tm}$ is a registered trademark of Mulberry Square Productions, Inc.

The Soul of a Horse is a registered trademark of Camp Horse Camp LLC

ABOUT JOE CAMP

Joe Camp, the man who created the floppy-eared superstar Benji, and wrote and directed all of his movies, believes that anything is possible if you work hard enough and have faith in yourself and in God. He was told by industry "experts" not to bother with the original Benji film; that it wouldn't work. But Joe didn't listen. He wrote, produced, and directed *Benji* from his Mulberry Square Productions office in Dallas, Texas. When completed, the film was turned down by every major film distributor in Hollywood, so Joe and his partner Ed Vanston had to form their own distribution company and release the picture themselves with Joe personally developing the marketing strategy, writing advertising copy and press releases, and supervising each and every booking. The rest is what they call, "history."

Joe has written (or co-written), produced and directed seven theatrical motion pictures cumulatively grossing over 200 million dollars, making him one of the most successful independent filmmakers of all time... the hard way, with family movies.

Joe is also author of the best selling book *The Soul of a Horse – Life Lessons from the Herd*, *The Soul of a Horse Blogged – The Journey Continues*, *Who Needs Hollywood*, and numerous children's books.

He is particularly proud of the difference he and his late wife, Carolyn, have made working with the Piney Woods School in Mississippi. This historically black boarding school educates mostly high risk kids from families below the poverty level, yet usually sends 100% of its graduates to college, often on full scholarship and financial aid. With Joe and Carolyn's help, many Piney Woods graduates have attended some of the best colleges and universities in the country, like Princeton, Harvard, Smith, Williams, Middlebury, Northwestern, Amherst, Emory

60

and Spelman. "Of all I've done," says Camp, "I'm most proud of the things we've accomplished for these kids. And the rewards are the greatest."

Joe embarked upon a national search for the new Benji in animal shelters across the country because the American Humane Association had announced that the original Benji's rescue from a shelter had caused more than one million adoptions. Since the search, Benji has generated more than a billion media exposures for shelters and rescue groups all across the nation. And has increased adoptions wherever she goes.

Over the years, Joe has been the subject of television, radio and newspaper interviews in more than 100 U.S. cities and several of the international capitals of the world. He has appeared on Good Morning America, Primetime Thursday, The Today Show, Fox and Friends, Hannity & Colmes, CNN, various awards shows, Entertainment Tonight, and on and on,, but today he is still in awe of his own success. "Inside, I'm still a kid sitting in a dark theater in Little Rock, Arkansas, watching Disney's *Song of the South* with happy tears rolling down my cheeks," says Camp. "To be able to bring that feeling to others is very special."

At this writing, Joe and his wife Kathleen have added horses to their many dogs and cats and are neck-deep in the new natural, *humane* horse movement.

Asked recently what he would like Benji's legacy to be, he was quick to respond, "The same as mine. To make a positive difference; to leave this planet better than we found it."

TAKE THE BENJI METHOD WITH VIDEO WHEREVER YOU GO!

Joe and Benji have produced an hour-and-twenty-minute demonstration video covering everything in this book. The Kindle edition of this book contains live links to that video right in the book! You can have this book and the video demonstrations with you wherever you're training. Go to Amazon.com or www.thebenjimethod.com

To order just the video downloaded to your computer **please visit: www.thebenjimethod.com**

SEND US **YOUR** VIDEOS

Send us a video of a family member and your pup doing any of the exercises in this book and we'll post it on The Benji Method Channel on YouTube and select one every month to be posted on the home page of our website and actually be in the eBook from that day forward! **Visit www.thebenjimethod.com for details.**

SEE ALL OF JOE CAMP'S BOOKS

www.14handspress.com

FOR MORE ON BENJI OR JOE CAMP

www.benji.com

www.benji.com/index2

www.thesoulofahorse.com

http://thesoulofahorse.com/blog

Send comments or questions to Joe:

joe@benji.com

Also by Joe Camp

The Soul of a Horse
Life Lessons from the Herd

The Soul of a Horse Blogged
The Journey Continues

Who Needs Hollywood
The Amazing Story of a Small Time Filmmaker
Who Writes the Screenplay, Raises the Production Budget,
Directs, and Distributes the #3 Movie of the Year

Coming

Born To Be Wild
The Soul of a Horse

The Soul of a Happier Healthier Horse
No Stalls - No Shoes - No Sugar

For more: www.14handspress.com

What Readers and Critics Are Saying About Joe Camp

"Joe Camp is a master storyteller." THE NEW YORK TIMES

"Joe Camp is a gifted storyteller and the results are magical. Joe entertains, educates and empowers, baring his own soul while articulating keystone principles of a modern revolution in horsemanship." RICK LAMB, AUTHOR AND TV/RADIO HOST "THE HORSE SHOW"

"This book is fantastic It has given me shivers, made me laugh and cry, and I just can't seem to put it down!" CHERYL PANNIER, WHO RADIO AM 1040 DES MOINES

"One cannot help but be touched by Camp's love and sympathy for animals and by his eloquence on the subject." MICHAEL KORDA, THE WASHINGTON POST

"Joe Camp is a natural when it comes to understanding how animals tick and a genius at telling us their story. His books are must-reads for those who love animals of any species." MONTY ROBERTS, AUTHOR OF NEW YORK TIMES BEST-SELLER THE MAN WHO LISTENS TO HORSES

"The tightly written, simply designed, and powerfully drawn chapters often read like short stories that flow from the heart. Camp has become something of a master at telling us what can be learned from animals, in this case specifically horses, without making us realize we have been educated, and, that is, perhaps, the mark of a real teacher." JACK L. KENNEDY, THE JOPLIN INDEPENDENT

"This book is absolutely fabulous! An amazing, amazing book. You're going to love it." Janet Parshall's America

"Joe speaks a clear and simple truth that grabs hold of your heart." YVONNE WELZ, EDITOR, THE HORSE'S HOOF MAGAZINE

"I wish you could *hear* my excitement for Joe Camp's new book. It is unique, powerful, needed." DR. MARTY BECKER, BEST-SELLING AUTHOR OF SEVERAL CHICKEN SOUP FOR THE SOUL BOOKS AND POPULAR VETERINARY CONTRIBUTOR TO ABC'S GOOD MORNING AMERICA

"I got my book yesterday and hold Joe Camp responsible for my bloodshot eyes. I couldn't put it down and morning came early!!! Joe transports me into his words. I feel like I am right there sharing his experiences. And his love for not just horses, but all of God's critters pours out from every page." *RUTH SWANDER – READER*

"I love this book! It is so hard to put it down, but I also don't want to read it too fast. I don't want it to end! Every person who loves an animal must have this book. I can't wait for the next one !!!!!!!!!" *NINA BLACK REID – READER*

"I LOVED the book! I had it read in 2 days. I had to make myself put it down. Joe and Kathleen have brought so much light to how horses should be treated and cared for. Again, thank you!" *ANITA LARGE - READER*

"LOVE the new book... reading it was such an emotional journey. Joe Camp is a gifted writer." *MARYKAY THUL LONGACRE - READER*

"I was actually really sad, when I got to the last page, because I was looking forward to picking it up every night." *SABINE REYNOSO - READER*

"*The Soul of a Horse Blogged* is insightful, enlightening, emotionally charged, hilarious, packed with wonderfully candid photography, and is masterfully woven by a consummate storyteller. Wonderful reading!" *HARRY H. MACDONALD - READER*

"I simply love the way Joe Camp writes. He stirs my soul. This is a must read book for everyone." *DEBBIE K - READER*

"This book swept me away. From the first to last page I felt transported! It's clever, witty, inspiring and a very fast read. I was sad when I finished it because I wanted to read more!" *DEBBIE CHARTRAND - READER*

"This book is an amazing, touching insight into Joe and Kathleen's personal journey that has an even more intimate feel than Joe's first best seller." *KATHERINE BOWEN – READER*

Notes

Made in United States
Orlando, FL
04 May 2022

17498760R00037